12 Days of Christmas Story Stones: Nativity Hands-On Bible Study
by Ashley Kersh
Faithful Little Hands
P.O. Box 19375
Denver, CO 80219

https://faithfullittlehands.com

© 2017 Ashley Kersh

join the community

We believe that learning, encouragement and growth happen best within a community. That's why we've created ways for you to connect with us and other families as you go through this study.

JOIN THE FACEBOOK GROUP

As soon as you have your hands on this study join the Facebook group: Faithful Families. There you will find encouragement, prayer, and connection to other families going through this study together. Post pictures, share insight and stories, and encourage others along the way.

https://www.facebook.com/groups/faithfulfamiliescommunity/

#FaithfulFamilies

Join the conversation on social media by using #faithfulfamilies. Start by letting us know when you have your copy of this book!

Facebook: https://www.facebook.com/faithfullittlehands
Instagram: https://www.instagram.com/faithfullittlehands
Twitter: https://www.twitter.com/faithfullittleh
Questions? Email us anytime at contactus@faithfullittlehands.com

how to use this book

Start a new family tradition this holiday season with Christmas story stones. Follow the nativity story through hands-on activities and family Bible study.

BIBLE STUDY

This Bible study can be done with kids of any age. It can be completed in 12 days or stretched out over the advent season by doing one lesson every other day. Use story stones to provide a visual, hands-on way for kids to remember each part of the story. Each lesson comes with a scripture passage, an ornament, discussion questions and additional activities.

NATIVITY STORY STONES

Start this study by making 12 Christmas story stones as outlined in this book. Each of the stones accompanies one of the 12 Bible lessons following the nativity story. You can make them all at once or make one each day. Feel free to follow the drawing tutorials or come up with your own designs.

READ AND DISCUSS

Each lesson contains a Bible verse, a suggested passage to read together and discussion questions. The discussion questions start with simple questions for younger children and progress to deeper questions for older children and adults.

ADDITIONAL ACTIVITIES

Each lesson ends with additional activities you can do as a family. These ideas begin with simple activities for younger children and progress to deeper activities for older children and adults. They include songs, crafts, family outings, and Bible study prompts.

ORNAMENTS

Included with each lesson are hand-drawn ornaments you can photocopy or print, color, and hang on your tree. Each ornament corresponds with one of the 12 Bible lessons. If you would like to reuse these ornaments each year you can laminate them. You can also buy blank wooden ornaments from an arts and crafts store and adhere the pictures with Mod Podge.

SCRIPTURE CARDS

At the end of the book are scripture cards with Bible verses from each day of the study. They can be printed or photocopied and used for teaching or scripture memory.

You can download a printable PDF version of the ornaments and scripture cards from the Faithful Families Facebook group.

How to make
story stones

MATERIALS

- 12 smooth river stones
- 1 white fine-tip oil-based paint marker
- Rubbing alcohol
- Q-tips

INSTRUCTIONS

- Follow the directions on the paint marker to get it started. Test it out on scrap paper until it draws smoothly.
- Draw a picture on each stone to correspond with the 12-day nativity story listed on the next page. Feel free to follow the drawing tutorials or draw them your own way.
- Make a mistake? Use rubbing alcohol and a Q-tip to erase the paint.
- Let the stones dry.
- Keep your stones in a draw string bag to use next year!

All materials can be found at most arts and crafts stores.

12 days of Christmas
story stones

Day 1: An Angel
Day 2: Mary
Day 3: Joseph
Day 4: Emmanuel
Day 5: Bethlehem
Day 6: A Stable

Day 7: A Manger
Day 8: Shepherds
Day 9: Angels Singing
Day 10: Wisemen
Day 11: A Star
Day 12: Gifts

Story stones tutorials

EMMANUEL   EMMANUEL

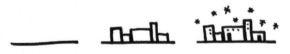 

Story stones tutorials

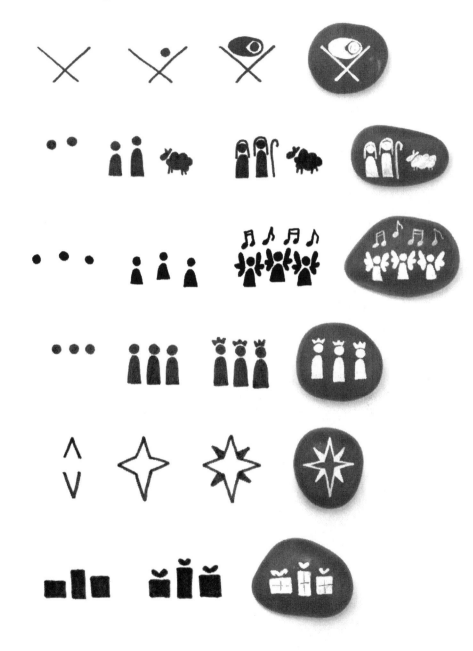

day one

an angel appears

LUKE 1:26

In the sixth month the angel Gabriel was sent from God to a city of Galilee named Nazareth.

READ

Luke 1:26-38

DISCUSS

- What was the name of the angel who visited Mary?
- Where did the angel come from?
- How would you have felt in Mary's position?
- Why do you think God chose to send an angel to bring the news of Jesus?

ACTIVITIES

- Color and hang the angel ornament.
- Make an angel craft.
- Sing or listen to the hymn "The Angel Gabriel from Heaven Came."
- Study other times that the angel Gabriel appeared in the Bible.

day two

Mary listens

LUKE 1:38

And Mary said, "Behold, I am the servant of the Lord; let it be to me according to your word."

READ

Luke 1:26-38, 46-55

DISCUSS

- What did the angel say to Mary?
- How did Mary respond to the news she had received?
- What did the angel say to reassure Mary?
- How did Mary show that she trusted the Lord?
- What stood out to you in Mary's song of praise?

ACTIVITIES

- Color and hang the Mary ornament.
- Sing or listen to the song "Mary Did You Know?"
- Write a prayer of praise for the things God has done in your own life.
- Study the life of Mary throughout the New Testament.

day three

Joseph follows

MATTHEW 1:24

When Joseph woke from sleep, he did as the angel of the Lord commanded him.

READ

Matthew 1:18-25

DISCUSS

- Who is Joseph?
- How did Joseph initially respond to Mary's news?
- What helped Joseph to trust God?
- Why do you think the angel appeared to Joseph in a dream?
- What is the significance of Joseph's lineage (son of David)?

ACTIVITIES

- Color and hang the Joseph ornament.
- Sing or listen to the song "This is All I Have to Give" by Todd Agnew.
- Draw or paint a picture of Joseph's dream.
- Study the lineage of Jesus listed in the book of Matthew.

day four

a prophecy fulfilled

MATTHEW 1:22-23

All this took place to fulfill what the Lord had spoken by the prophet: "Behold, the virgin shall conceive and bear a son, and they shall call his name Immanuel" (which means, God with us).

READ

Matthew 1:20-23, Isaiah 7:14

DISCUSS

- Who was "Emmanuel" and what does "Emmanuel" mean?
- Why do you think this was revealed to Joseph?
- Why do you think "Emmanuel" was one of the first names of Jesus revealed in the New Testament?

ACTIVITIES

- Color and hang the Emmanuel ornament.
- Sing or listen to the song "O Come, O Come, Emmanuel."
- Research and make a list of the names of Jesus.
- Study other Old Testament prophecies that were fulfilled by the life of Jesus.

day five

to Bethlehem

LUKE 2:4

And Joseph also went up from Galilee, from the town of Nazareth, to Judea, to the city of David, which is called Bethlehem, because he was of the house and lineage of David.

READ

Luke 2:1-5

DISCUSS

- What was the name of the city in which Jesus was born?
- Why did Joseph and Mary go to Bethlehem?
- How do you imagine they felt going on such a journey?
- Why is Bethlehem called the "City of David"?

ACTIVITIES

- Color and hang the Bethlehem ornament.
- Sing or listen to "O Little Town of Bethlehem."
- Go on a hike or drive and reflect on Mary and Joseph's journey.
- Research the journey of Mary and Joseph from Nazareth to Bethlehem.

day six

a place to stay

LUKE 2:7

And she gave birth to her firstborn son and wrapped him in swaddling clothes and laid him in a manger, because there was no place for them in the inn.

READ

Luke 2:1-7

DISCUSS

- Where was Jesus born?
- Why wasn't there room for Mary and Joseph to stay at the inn?
- How do you think Mary and Joseph felt having a baby in a stable?
- Why do you think God planned for Jesus to arrive in this way?

ACTIVITIES

- Color and hang the stable ornament.
- Sing or listen to "Away in a Manger."
- Put together a family nativity set.
- Visit a farm or local shelter.

day seven

a child is born

ISAIAH 9:6

For to us a child is born, to us a son is given; and the government shall be upon his shoulder, and his name shall be called Wonderful Counselor, Mighty God, Everlasting Father, Price of Peace.

READ

Isaiah 9:2-7

DISCUSS

- Who is the child in this passage?
- What names of Jesus are given in this passage?
- What do each of these names mean?
- What else does this passage seem to say about Jesus?

ACTIVITIES

- Color and hang the baby Jesus ornament.
- Sing or listen to the song "Joy to the World."
- Make ornaments for the different names of Jesus.
- Study the ways that Jesus fulfilled the prophecies in Isaiah 9.

day eight

shepherds hear

LUKE 2:8

And in the same region there were shepherds out in the field, keeping watch over their flock by night.

READ

Luke 2:8-12

DISCUSS

- What did the angel say to the shepherds?
- How did the shepherds feel when the angel appeared?
- Why do you think God revealed the birth of Jesus to shepherds?
- What other shepherds are mentioned throughout the Bible?

ACTIVITIES

- Color and hang the shepherds ornament.
- Sing or listen to the song "What Child is This?"
- Make a sheep craft.
- Study the role of shepherds throughout the Bible.

day nine

angels sing

LUKE 2:13-14

And suddenly there was with the angel a multitude of the heavenly host praising God and saying, "Glory to God in the highest, and on earth peace among those with whom he is pleased."

READ

Luke 2:13-20

DISCUSS

- How many angels were praising God?
- Why do you think so many angels appeared?
- How do you think the shepherds felt in that moment?
- What other times do angels appear in the Bible?

ACTIVITIES

- Color and hang the angels ornament.
- Sing or listen to "Hark the Harold Angels Sing."
- Make a homemade musical instrument.
- Go Christmas caroling or attend a Christmas concert.

day ten

wisemen come

MATTHEW 2:1

Now after Jesus was born in Bethlehem of Judea in the days of Herod the king, behold, wise men from the east came to Jerusalem.

READ

Matthew 2:1-9

DISCUSS

- Who are the wisemen?
- How did the wisemen hear about Jesus?
- Why did the king want them to find Jesus?
- How did the wisemen know where to go?
- Why do you think God revealed the birth of Jesus in this way?

ACTIVITIES

- Color and hang the wisemen ornament.
- Make and decorate paper crowns.
- Sing or listen to "We Three Kings."
- Study the culture of Jerusalem at the time of the birth of Jesus.

day eleven

a star appears

MATTHEW 2:9b

And behold, the star they had seen when it rose went before them until it came over the place where the child was.

READ

Matthew 2:1-12

DISCUSS

- How did the wisemen know where to find Jesus?
- When did the star appear?
- Why did the wisemen want to see Jesus?
- Why do you think God used a star to lead them to Jesus?

ACTIVITIES

- Color and hang the star ornament.
- Sing or listen to the song "O Holy Night"
- Make paper stars.
- Hang Christmas lights or visit a Christmas lights display.
- Research theories about the stars at the time of Jesus' birth.

day twelve

gifts of worship

MATTHEW 2:11b

Then, opening their treasures, they offered him gifts, gold and frankincense and myrrh.

READ

Matthew 2:10-12

DISCUSS

- What gifts did the wisemen give to Jesus?
- Why did the wisemen give gifts?
- Why do you think the wisemen gave gold, frankincense and myrrh?
- What are ways we can worship God through giving?

ACTIVITIES

- Color and hang the gifts ornament.
- Sing or listen to the song "O Come All Ye Faithful."
- Make Christmas cards to give to friends and family.
- Donate items to a local charity.
- Study what the Bible teaches about giving.

Scripture cards

An angel appears

LUKE 1:26

In the sixth month the angel Gabriel was sent from God to a city of Galilee named Nazareth.

Mary listens

LUKE 1:38

And Mary said, "Behold, I am the servant of the Lord; let it be to me according to your word."

Joseph follows

MATTHEW 1:24

When Joseph woke from sleep, he did as the angel of the Lord commanded him.

A prophecy fulfilled

MATTHEW 1:22-23

All this took place to fulfill what the Lord had spoken by the prophet: "Behold, the virgin shall conceive and bear a son, and they shall call his name Immanuel" (which means, God with us).

To Bethlehem

LUKE 2:4

And Joseph also went up from Galilee, from the town of Nazareth, to Judea, to the city of David, which is called Bethlehem, because he was of the house and lineage of David.

A place to stay

LUKE 2:7

And she gave birth to her firstborn son and wrapped him in swaddling clothes and laid him in a manger, because there was no place for them in the inn.

A child is born

ISAIAH 9:6

For to us a child is born, to us a son is given; and the government shall be upon his shoulder, and his name shall be called Wonderful Counselor, Mighty God, Everlasting Father, Price of Peace.

Shepherds hear

LUKE 2:8

And in the same region there were shepherds out in the field, keeping watch over their flock by night.

Angels sing

LUKE 2:13-14

And suddenly there was with the angel a multitude
of the heavenly host praising God and saying,
"Glory to God in the highest, and on earth peace
among those with whom he is pleased."

Wisemen come

MATTHEW 2:1

Now after Jesus was born in Bethlehem
of Judea in the days of Herod the king, behold,
wise men from the east came to Jerusalem.

A star appears

MATTHEW 2:9b

And behold, the star they had seen when it rose went before them until it came over the place where the child was.

Gifts of worship

MATTHEW 2:11b

Then, opening their treasures, they offered him gifts, gold and frankincense and myrrh.

Notes

stay in touch

SUBSCRIBE TO OUR NEWSLETTER

Stay up to date with our latest faith-based crafts, activities, and resources by signing up for our email list.

https://faithfullittlehands.com/subscribe

JOIN THE FACEBOOK GROUP

Connect with a community of families as we teach our children about Jesus. You'll find encouragement, prayer, and inspiration from others when you join Faithful Families.

https://www.facebook.com/groups/faithfulfamiliescommunity

FOLLOW OUR BLOG

Throughout the year we find creative ways to teach our kids the Bible. We use everything from crafts to science experiments to help our kids grow in their faith. Follow along with us on our blog, Faithful Little Hands.

Blog: https://faithfullittlehands.com
Facebook: https://www.facebook.com/faithfullittlehands
Instagram: https://www.instagram.com/faithfullittlehands
Twitter: https://www.twitter.com/faithfullittleh
Pinterest: https://www.pinterest.com/faithfullittlehands

Made in the USA
Lexington, KY
18 November 2017